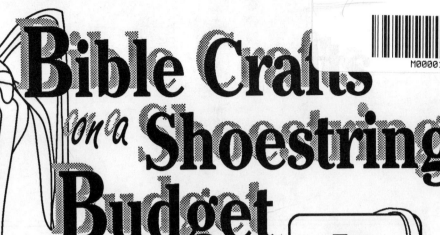

Bible Crafts on a Shoestring Budget

For Ages 2 & 3

Publisher	*Arthur L. Miley*
Author	*Wanda Pelfrey*
Managing Editor	*Jack Cavanaugh*
Editorial Director	*Carol Rogers*
Art Director	*Deborah Birch*
Production Assistant	*Chris D. Neynaber*
Illustrator	*Fran Kizer*
Proofreader	*Grace Mainhood*

Rainbow BOOKS

Copyright 1994 • Second Printing
Rainbow Books • P.O. Box 261129 • San Diego, CA 92196

#RB36126
ISBN 0-937282-08-1

Lovingly dedicated to my parents, Ogden and Doris Barker, whose 50th wedding anniversary coincides with the completion of this book.

Wanda Pelfrey

INTRODUCTION

Learning about God and His Word should be the joyful right of every child. *Bible Crafts on a Shoestring Budget for Ages 2 & 3* contains 30 creative crafts designed to provide happy learning experiences for 2s and 3s for very little financial expense.

Making Bible crafts can be a valuable teaching tool as well as a fun and meaningful way for children to remember the stories of the Bible. Each Bible craft begins with a brief introduction explaining how the craft relates to the Bible lesson. The memory verse words (from the King James Version unless otherwise noted) help reinforce the Bible story or biblical concept. Ideas for guided conversation and ways to use the completed project in class or at home appear at the end of each craft. Always make a sample craft prior to the children's session so that you understand each step involved. Safety should be a priority. Do not let children handle staplers or scissors or other sharp objects. Close supervision is recommended at all times.

This book is intended to make every craft session fun for the teacher! The section labeled BEFORE CLASS gives clear instructions for any advance preparation required, WHAT YOU NEED lists all materials needed to complete the craft, and WHAT TO DO leads you step-by-step through the craft making process. Guided conversation suggestions and learning activity ideas are highlighted with the symbol *, and include ways to encourage the children to apply the biblical concepts to their own lives.

These Bible crafts are divided into the following categories:
- Crafts About God's Creation
- Bible Story Crafts
- Crafts About Jesus' Life and Teachings
- Crafts to Help Me Learn to Worship
- Crafts for Special Times

Each craft in this book can be completed on a shoestring budget. The pages are perforated for easy removal so that instructions and patterns may be reproduced. Inexpensive school supplies and household materials such as cereal boxes, fabric scraps, and drinking straws help keep expenses to a minimum. A reproducible NOTE TO FAMILIES, requesting their help in acquiring supplies, is included on page 7. Send a note home two or three weeks before your first craft session so parents and friends can begin collecting odds and ends for your collection.

These Bible crafts are designed for use in a variety of sessions including Sunday school, vacation Bible school, Christian day school, Wednesday night activities, or at any other time when the Bible is being taught. Use *Bible Crafts on a Shoestring Budget* to share effectively the excitement about the Good News found in every Bible story — the news of God's wonder-filled love for us all!

CONTENTS

MEMORY VERSE INDEX

REPRODUCIBLE NOTE
TO FAMILIES

For your convenience, the following page contains notes to families, requesting their help in collecting the materials necessary to complete the crafts. Hand out these notes two or three weeks before you need the items. Specify whether items should be brought in at any time or only on a specific date. Then simply duplicate the notes, cut them apart, and send one home with each child.

To Families of Two- and Three-Year-Olds

We are planning many special craft activities for your child. Some of these crafts include regular household materials. We would like to ask your help in saving the items checked below for our activities:

- ☐ 2 and 3-liter plastic bottles
- ☐ brown paper sacks, lunch size
- ☐ cardboard or plastic containers with lids
- ☐ cereal boxes
- ☐ chenille wire
- ☐ old crayons
- ☐ cross stitch material scraps
- ☐ dish detergent bottles, plastic
- ☐ dried beans
- ☐ embroidery floss
- ☐ fabric scraps
- ☐ felt
- ☐ fusible web
- ☐ ink pads
- ☐ small jingle bells

- ☐ plastic jars with lids (peanut butter jar size)
- ☐ plastic lids from margarine tubs
- ☐ polyester stuffing
- ☐ old printed music
- ☐ scraps of fusible web
- ☐ spray can caps
- ☐ 4 1/2-inch cardboard tubes
- ☐ paper clips
- ☐ plastic drinking straws
- ☐ plastic sandwich bags
- ☐ toothpaste boxes, cardboard
- ☐ trash bag ties
- ☐ used fabric softener sheets
- ☐ yarn

Please bring the items on _____   **Thank you for your help!**

To Families of Two- and Three-Year-Olds

We are planning many special craft activities for your child. Some of these crafts include regular household materials. We would like to ask your help in saving the items checked below for our activities:

- ☐ 2 and 3-liter plastic bottles
- ☐ brown paper sacks, lunch size
- ☐ cardboard or plastic containers with lids
- ☐ cereal boxes
- ☐ chenille wire
- ☐ old crayons
- ☐ cross stitch material scraps
- ☐ dish detergent bottles, plastic
- ☐ dried beans
- ☐ embroidery floss
- ☐ fabric scraps
- ☐ felt
- ☐ fusible web
- ☐ ink pads
- ☐ small jingle bells

- ☐ plastic jars with lids (peanut butter jar size)
- ☐ plastic lids from margarine tubs
- ☐ polyester stuffing
- ☐ old printed music
- ☐ scraps of fusible web
- ☐ spray can caps
- ☐ 4 1/2-inch cardboard tubes
- ☐ paper clips
- ☐ plastic drinking straws
- ☐ plastic sandwich bags
- ☐ toothpaste boxes, cardboard
- ☐ trash bag ties
- ☐ used fabric softener sheets
- ☐ yarn

Please bring the items on _____   **Thank you for your help!**

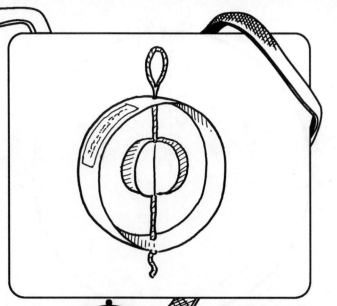

God's World Art

Use this window hanging to help children realize that only God can create something from nothing.

MEMORY VERSE

God created...the earth.

— Genesis 1:1

WHAT TO DO

1. Help each child slip a green and blue construction paper circle together to form a 3-D world.
2. Help each child thread a piece of yarn through the two holes in his plastic ring. Secure each end with a paper clip.
3. Place a small amount of glue along the middle of the yarn.
4. Help each child place his blue and green world on the yarn so the yarn fits between one blue and one green section.
5. Tell each child to hold his world in place for a few seconds.
6. Tie a hanging loop in the top of the yarn.
7. Help each child glue a memory verse onto the plastic ring, reading the words as you do so.

✱ When the craft is finished, say, **We made these world hangings from paper, plastic, and yarn. We used our hands. God spoke and made the world from nothing. We say God created the world.**

BEFORE CLASS

Cut the bottom off a 2-liter plastic soda bottle. Cut the remaining bottle at 1 1/2-inch intervals to form rings. You will need one ring for each child. Punch two holes opposite one another across the plastic ring. Cut one blue and one green construction paper circle for each child, using the pattern on page 10. Cut a center line in each circle, as marked.

Cut a 12-inch piece of yarn for each child. Knot one end of each piece of yarn.

WHAT YOU NEED

- ☐ circle and memory verse patterns from page 10
- ☐ blue construction paper
- ☐ green construction paper
- ☐ a 2-liter plastic bottle for every four children
- ☐ yarn, 1 foot per child
- ☐ paper clips, 2 per child
- ☐ scissors

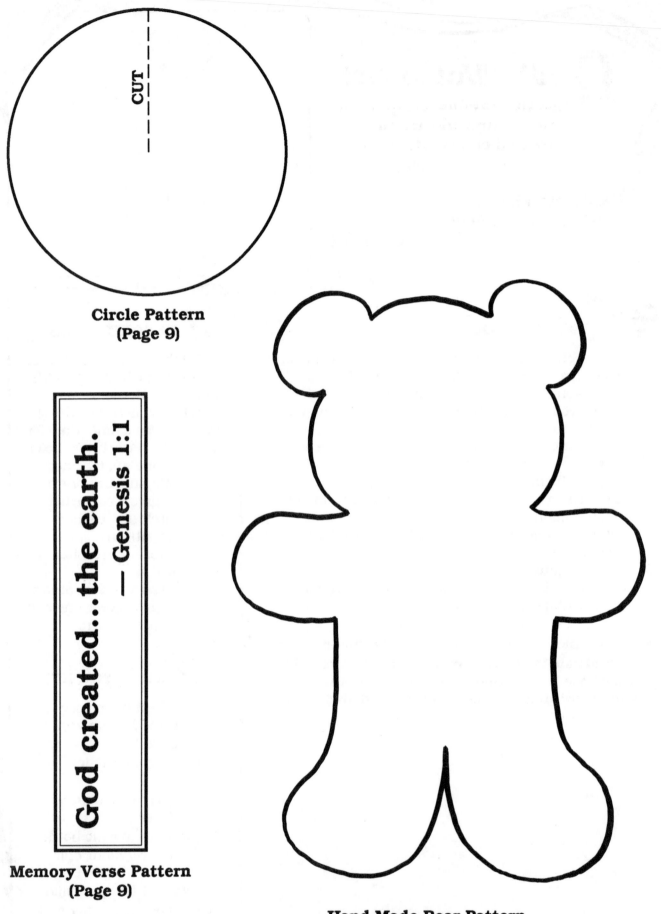

Circle Pattern
(Page 9)

God created...the earth.
— Genesis 1:1

CUT

Memory Verse Pattern
(Page 9)

Hand Made Bear Pattern
(Page 11)

Hand Made Bear

Use this lovable, stuffed bear to help the children realize that God created all animals.

MEMORY VERSE

God made the wild animals.
— Genesis 1:25 (NIV)

WHAT TO DO

1. Show the children a finished bear.
2. Demonstrate how to place the stuffing in the opening.
3. Working one on one, help each child place stuffing in the bear. You may have to hold the opening open for younger children.
4. Stitch the opening to close. Do not let the children touch the needles or scissors.

✱ As you stitch each child's bear, say, **When God made animals He did not use fabric and stuffing. He simply spoke and they were formed. We cannot do that, so we use fabric and stuffing. God also made animals so they can have baby animals just like themselves. Let's thank God for animals.** Say a brief prayer. Then say the memory verse together.

TIP: Old nylons may be used for soft, durable stuffing material. Snip the nylons into small, easily manageable shapes and sizes.

BEFORE CLASS

Using the bear pattern on page 10, cut two fabric pieces for each child. Be sure to make extras for unexpected visitors. You can use different fabrics for different children's bears.

Stitch the two fabric pieces together, leaving a 1 1/2-inch opening along one side.

WHAT YOU NEED

- ☐ scraps of soft fabric
- ☐ sewing machine (optional)
- ☐ needle & thread
- ☐ polyester stuffing
- ☐ threaded needle in classroom
- ☐ scissors

God Made Me

The children will feel important that God created them. Help them realize that God made each person unique.

MEMORY VERSE

It is He Who made us.
— Psalm 100:3 (NIV)

BEFORE CLASS

Contact a parent of each child and ask that they send a small snapshot of the child to class. Tell them it will be returned in an altered condition.

Using the patterns from below, cut one poster board frame and one paper memory verse for each child. Fold the poster board in half and place the pattern on the fold before cutting.

WHAT YOU NEED

☐ duplicated pattern from below
☐ light color of poster board
☐ small snapshot of each child
☐ ink pad
☐ gluestick
☐ scissors
☐ damp paper towels for clean up

 WHAT TO DO

1. Give each child a poster board frame. Help each one glue his picture to the inside of the frame so the poster board frames the picture. (Trim the snapshot, if necessary.)
2. Working one on one, help each child put thumbprints around the frame using the stamp pad. Place damp paper towels next to each child. Help the children clean their hands thoroughly before handling the memory verse.
3. As you work, say, **Did you know that God makes each person different? Even twins who look alike have different fingerprints. No one else is just like you.**
4. Put glue inside the frame and help each child attach the memory verse .
5. Read the memory verse with the children. Help them repeat it with you.

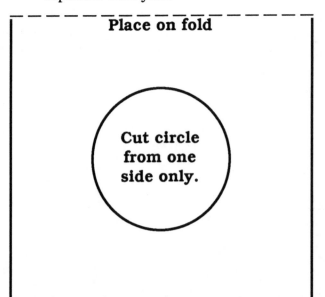

Place on fold

Cut circle from one side only.

It is He Who made us.
— Psalm 100:3 (NIV)

A Happy Tree

Use the story of Zacchaeus to show how Jesus loved Zacchaeus. Help each child learn that God loves him also.

MEMORY VERSE

He...welcomed Him gladly.
— Luke 19:6 (NIV)

BEFORE CLASS

Cut one tree, one memory verse, and one Zacchaeus for each child using the patterns on page 14. Cut or tear green construction paper or tissue paper into small pieces.

Punch two small holes where indicated on Zacchaeus and tree figures. Place an 18-inch length of floss or yarn in the holes of each Zacchaeus figure. Wrap a small piece of tape around each end of floss to stiffen.

WHAT YOU NEED

- [ ] patterns from page 14
- [ ] poster board
- [ ] scraps of green construction paper or tissue paper
- [ ] embroidery floss or yarn, 18 inches per child
- [ ] glue or paste
- [ ] hole punch
- [ ] tape

WHAT TO DO

1. Spread glue on the top portion of each child's tree.
2. Encourage the children to place pieces of green construction paper or tissue paper over the glue.
3. Spread glue near the bottom of each child's tree trunk.
4. Help the children place the memory verse over the glue on the tree trunk.
5. Briefly tell the story or sing a song about Zacchaeus (Luke 19:1-10) as the children work.
6. Help each child place the two ends of floss through the holes in his tree, so Zacchaeus is on the front of the tree. Tie the floss in back.
7. Show the children how to pull the yarn gently to make Zacchaeus climb the tree and then come down.

✱ Read the memory verse. Say, **Zacchaeus welcomed Jesus because he knew Jesus loved him. Each of us should be ready to welcome Jesus into our lives because Jesus loves each one of us.**

He...welcomed
Him gladly.

— Luke 19:6 (NIV)

God Cares Ark

This ark will teach the children that God's instructions should be obeyed.

MEMORY VERSE

Noah did everything just as God commanded him.

— Genesis 6:22 (NIV)

WHAT TO DO

1. Show the children a completed ark.
2. Let the children scribble color the manila or brown poster board pieces with brown crayons.
3. Place the paper arks face up, one in front of each child. Spread glue along the bottom edge of each pattern. Hand each child the bottom poster board piece of the ark. Help each child position his piece along the bottom of the paper ark.
4. Spread glue over the remainder of the bottom portion of the ark. Continue helping the children add ark pieces in order, from the bottom to the top. Hand them the appropriate poster board pieces one at a time.
5. On the top square area, place glue only around the edge, so the door will open.
6. Show the children how to open the door to see the animals inside.

* Hand each child three animal crackers. Let them eat one and place the other two in the ark as you briefly tell the story of Noah (Genesis 6-9). When God tells Noah to come out of the ark and bring out the animals, show the children how to open their arks and remove the animals. Let them eat the animals if they wish, as you tell them about God's promise of the rainbow. Compliment the children on carefully following your instructions. Say, **Noah was a careful carpenter. God cared about Noah. God gave Noah instructions that would keep him safe. Noah was safe because he carefully followed God's instructions.** Hand each child a plastic sandwich bag filled with two animal crackers to take home with the ark.

BEFORE CLASS

Duplicate the top ark pattern on page 16 for each child. Using the bottom ark for a pattern, cut a second ark in pieces for each child from poster board. The top piece may be cut from a bright color. The other pieces should be manila or brown. Keep each ark pattern and its poster board pieces separate from the others.

Place two animals crackers in a plastic sandwich bag for each child.

WHAT YOU NEED

- [ ] duplicated ark patterns from page 16
- [ ] manila or brown poster board
- [ ] brightly colored poster board (optional)
- [ ] brown crayons
- [ ] animal crackers, five for each child
- [ ] plastic sandwich bags
- [ ] glue

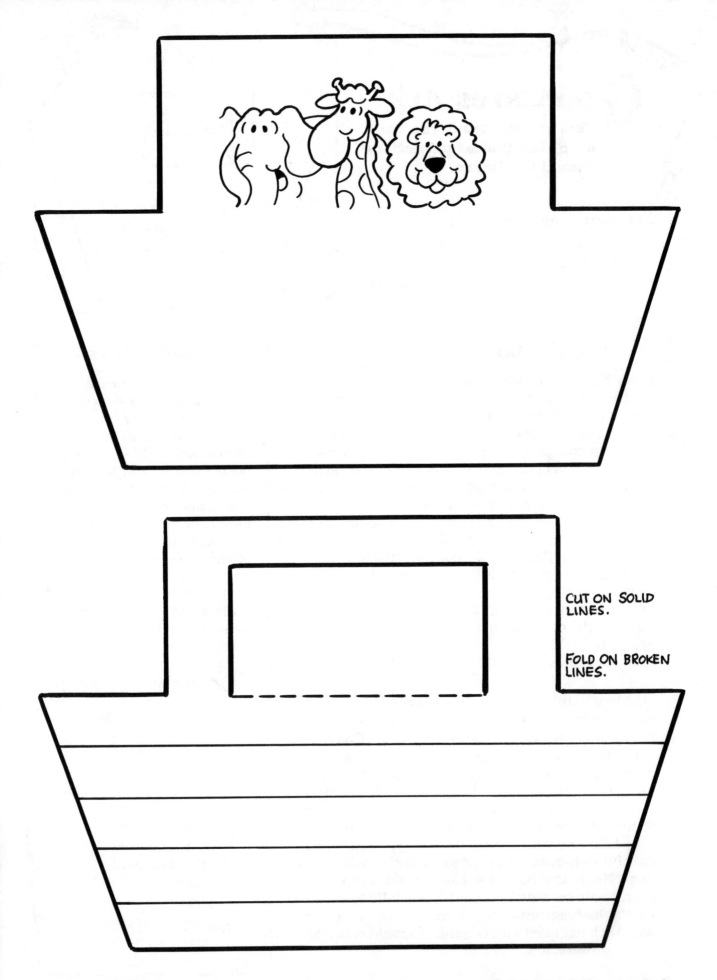

CUT ON SOLID
LINES.

FOLD ON BROKEN
LINES.

Bible Crafts On A Shoestring Budget

Special Banner

This banner will help each child realize that being part of a Christian home is a blessing.

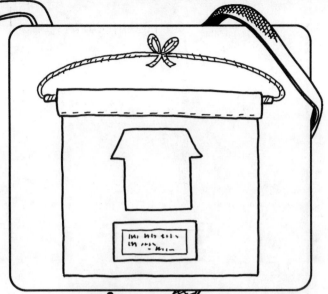

MEMORY VERSE

We will serve the Lord.

— Joshua 24:15

WHAT TO DO

1. Work one on one with each child and carefully guard the low heat iron. (Tape the iron on the low setting.) Let the child wear the mittens. Help the child iron a house and a rectangle onto the felt piece. Be sure the casing is at the top of the felt piece. Never leave the iron unattended.
2. When all children have ironed, disconnect the iron and move it to a safe place, out of the reach of the children.
3. Help each child glue the memory verse box onto the rectangular fabric on the banner.
4. Let each child push a straw through the casing at the top of the felt piece.
5. Help each child push his strip of yarn through the straw and tie it for him.

* Read the memory verse words. Say, **Joshua was a man who loved and served God. What a wonderful blessing it is to have parents who teach you God's ways.** Encourage the children to repeat the memory verse with you. Of course, you will want to be sensitive to any child who is not from a Christian home. Hold up the Christian home as the ideal.

BEFORE CLASS

Cut one 7 x 5-inch felt piece for each child using the pattern on page 18. Fold a narrow end of each piece over 1 inch. Sew it to form a casing. Leave the ends open. Cut a house and a rectangle from material scraps, using the patterns on page 18. Iron each cut piece to fusible web.

Duplicate and cut a verse pattern from page 18 for each child. Cut one 24-inch piece of yarn for each child. Wrap tape around one end of each yarn piece.

WHAT YOU NEED

- [ ] duplicated patterns from page 18
- [ ] 7 x 5-inch felt pieces
- [ ] textured material
- [ ] plastic straws
- [ ] yarn
- [ ] scraps of fusible web
- [ ] clear tape
- [ ] iron
- [ ] glue
- [ ] needle & thread
- [ ] a pair of child's mittens

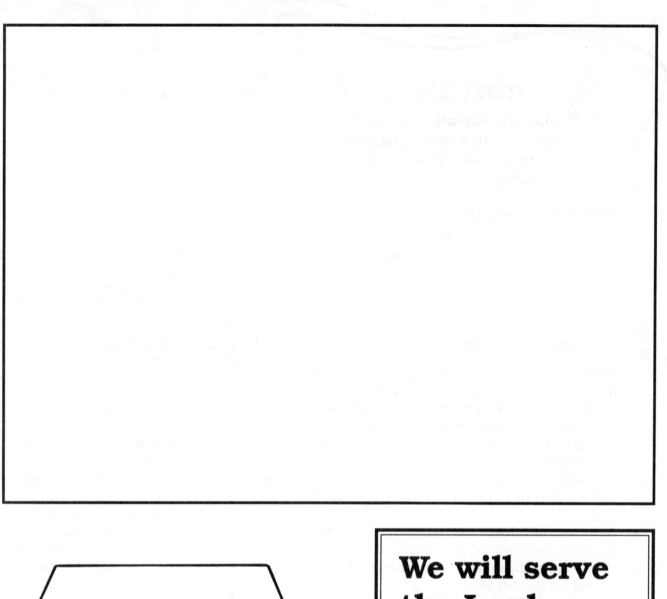

**We will serve
the Lord.**
— Joshua 24:15

A Colorful Coat

Making Joseph's coat will provide an opportunity to discuss envy, a troublesome feeling for most children.

MEMORY VERSE

His brethren envied him.

— Genesis 37:11

WHAT TO DO

1. Explain the safe use of the iron. Let each child wear the mittens while using the iron. Of course, an adult will be holding the iron at all times.
2. Working one on one, place the felt coat on a piece of typing paper.
3. Allow each child to sprinkle crayon shavings on his coat.
4. Cover the coat with another piece of typing paper.
5. Help the child iron over the top paper until crayon begins to melt through.
6. Remove the top paper and fold the felt in half to form a coat. (Do not iron the uncovered felt.)

✳ Let each child dress the Joseph figure in the coat as you tell the story of Joseph's gift from his father (Genesis 37). Lead the children to see that they should not envy the possessions of someone else. Say, **Joseph's brothers wanted his beautiful coat. Because they envied Joseph, they did a bad thing.** Have the children say the memory verse with you. Then say, **We should feel happy when our friends receive good things.**

TIP: Need a source of inexpensive, lightweight cardboard? Try empty cereal or pasta boxes. They are blank on one side. Many crafts calling for poster board can be made with cereal box cardboard.

BEFORE CLASS

Cut one coat from felt and one Joseph from poster board for each child. Grate several brightly colored crayons.

Locate a safe and sturdy place to use a slightly warm iron in your classroom. Tape the iron on the safe temperature. Assign one adult to stay with it at all times. Do not leave the iron unattended.

WHAT YOU NEED

- [ ] pattern from page 20
- [ ] white felt
- [ ] poster board
- [ ] old crayons
- [ ] typing paper
- [ ] warm iron
- [ ] tape
- [ ] a pair of child's mittens to fit the largest child's hands

Miriam 3-D

This craft will help the children understand that every job is an opportunity to do good.

MEMORY VERSE

Do good.

— Psalm 37:3

WHAT TO DO

1. Briefly tell the story of Miriam watching over Baby Moses (Exodus 2:1-8). You may prefer to read the story from a picture book.
2. Give each child a card to scribble color. Staple each card onto the top corner of a plastic sandwich bag. Cover the staple with a piece of tape to prevent scratching.
3. Write the child's name on the back of the card.
4. Say, **This card says, "Careful Miriam." Miriam had an important job to do. She was careful to do it well. This card also says, "Do good." These words are from Psalm 37:3 in the Bible.**
5. Give each child a cut out of Miriam, the grass, the water, and the basket, in that order. Help him arrange the pieces inside the sandwich bag as you repeat the story.
6. Help each child close the flap or zipper top on the sandwich bag.

✱ Say, **Our memory verse says, Do good. One way we can do good is to do every job we have the very best we can.** Ask the children to repeat the memory verse words with you.

BEFORE CLASS

Using the patterns from the following page, cut one of each of the following for each child: green grass, blue water, brown basket and Miriam.

Duplicate a box of words for each child. Fold the boxes in half to form cards with the words on the inside.

WHAT YOU NEED

- ☐ duplicated patterns from page 22
- ☐ plastic sandwich bags
- ☐ green construction paper
- ☐ blue construction paper
- ☐ brown construction paper
- ☐ stapler
- ☐ crayons
- ☐ tape

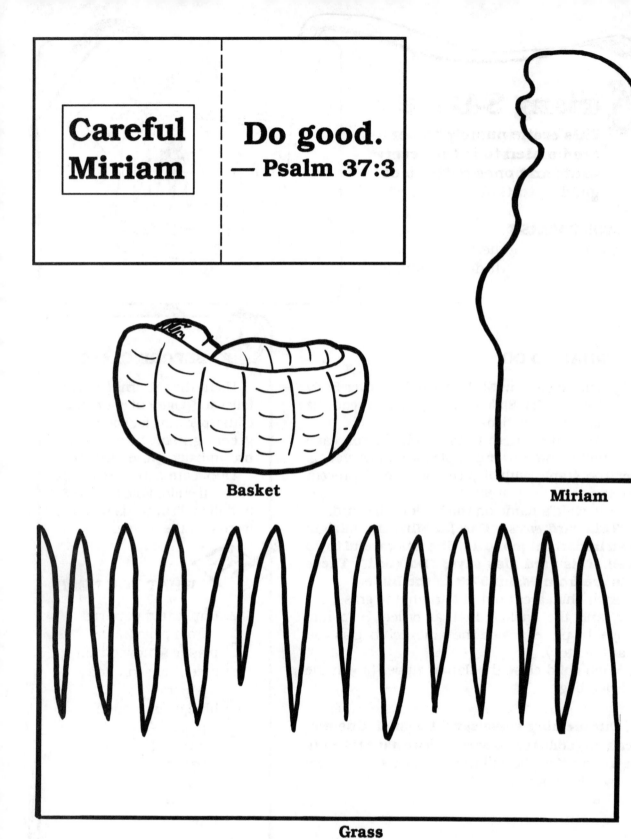

Careful Miriam

Do good.
— Psalm 37:3

Basket

Miriam

Grass

Water

Bible Crafts On A Shoestring Budget

Strong Samson

This bottle puppet of Samson can be used to introduce your little ones to the idea of looking to God for strength.

MEMORY VERSE

O Lord God, strengthen me.

　　　　　　　— Judges 16:28 (NIV)

WHAT TO DO

1. Give each child a 2-liter bottle. Let each child glue a Samson face on the plastic bottle. Make sure the neck of the bottle is at the bottom of the face.
2. Give each child eight strips of construction paper. Show the children how to glue strips of construction paper onto the bottom of the bottle to make hair.
3. Hand each child five or six yarn lengths. Show the children how to glue strips of yarn around the mouth of the puppet to make a beard.
4. Demonstrate how the puppet can be made to move by putting a finger into the bottle mouth.

✱ As the children play with their puppets, talk about how God made Samson strong as long as he continued to do what God had asked him to do. Tell the children they can find out what things God wants them to do in the Bible. Lead the children in praying for God to give them strength to do right things. Say, **God made Samson's body strong when Samson obeyed Him. God also gave Samson a different kind of strength. The strength to do the right thing.** Say the memory verse words with the children.

BEFORE CLASS

Make copies of Samson's face, one per child. Cut them out.

Cut strips of brown or black construction paper into 12-inch lengths, eight per child. Cut matching yarn into 2-inch lengths, five or six per child.

WHAT YOU NEED

- ☐ duplicated Samson face pattern from page 24, one per child
- ☐ empty 2-liter plastic bottles, one per child
- ☐ brown or black construction paper
- ☐ brown or black yarn
- ☐ glue

Zechariah

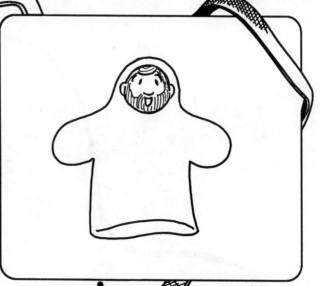

Use this hand puppet to help the children realize what a blessing it is to be able to praise God.

MEMORY VERSE

Praise be to the Lord.

— Luke 1:68 (NIV)

WHAT TO DO

1. Place glue on the back of each circle face.
2. Let each child put the face in place on the puppet.
3. While the glue dries say, **God gave Zechariah some exciting news. Then God took Zechariah's voice away while that news was happening. Zechariah could see God keeping His promise, but he could not praise God. When the promise was kept and Zechariah's son, John, was born, God gave Zechariah back his voice. How happy Zechariah was. He used his voice to praise God.**

* Tell the children the memory verse. Talk about the frustration Zechariah must have felt while he was mute and the joy he must have felt when his voice was returned. Say the memory verse again with the children. Say, **Those are some of the words Zechariah used to praise God.** Have the children repeat the words using their puppets.

BEFORE CLASS

Cut two pieces of felt for each child using the puppet pattern on page 26. Stitch the two sides together, leaving the bottom open. Cut one face circle for each child.

WHAT YOU NEED

- ☐ duplicated patterns from page 26
- ☐ felt
- ☐ light weight fabric
- ☐ needle & thread
- ☐ glue

Daniel's Den

Help the children act out the story of Daniel in the lions' den and impress upon them the importance of prayer.

MEMORY VERSE

He...prayed, giving thanks to his God.
— Daniel 6:10 (NIV)

WHAT TO DO

1. Give each child three lions and several brown fabric scraps. Spread glue on the lions and let the children place the fabric on top.
2. Help each child glue three lions around the inside of the plastic ring so the fabric is away from the plastic. Tell him he will have to hold the lions for a few seconds so they will stick.
3. Help the child glue the words "Daniel prays" near the top of the ring, and "God sent His angel..." near the bottom.
4. Briefly tell the story of Daniel in the lion's den (Daniel 6:1-27). Emphasize the fact that Daniel thought it was important to pray even when the king said not to. Explain that Daniel's safety was an answer to prayer.
5. Encourage the children to act out the story. As you tell it, they may put Daniel into the den and remove him.
6. Read the memory verse to the children. Ask them to say it with you.

TIP: Brown paper grocery sacks may be substituted for brown construction paper.

BEFORE CLASS

Cut the bottom off a 2- or 3-liter plastic bottle. Cut the bottle at 3 1/2-inch intervals to form rings. You will need one ring per child.

Trace the lion and Daniel patterns on page 28 onto brown construction paper and cut them out. You will need three lions and one Daniel per child.

Duplicate the words for each child, one of each word box for each child.

WHAT YOU NEED

- ☐ two- or three-liter plastic bottles
- ☐ brown construction paper
- ☐ patterns from page 28
- ☐ brown fabric scraps
- ☐ glue

Daniel prays.

God sent His angel and shut
the mouths of the lions.

Build a House

This house will help the children understand that the Bible teaches God's way is always the wise way.

MEMORY VERSE

The Lord gives wisdom.

— Proverbs 2:6 (NIV)

WHAT TO DO

1. Give each child a jar. Let each child pour 1/2 cup of sand or cornmeal into the jar.
2. Help the child screw the jar lid on tightly.
3. Show the children how to place the jar on it's side so the rock is on the bottom.
4. Help the child glue the house on the outside of the jar so it appears to be resting on top of the rock.
5. Demonstrate how to rock the jar back and forth. Ask, **Does the sand move? Does the rock move? Which would be better to build a house on?**
6. Say the memory verse. Ask the children to repeat it. Say, **God's Word never changes. It is like the rock. We can build our lives on God's Word.**

BEFORE CLASS

Hot glue one rock inside one side of each child's jar.

Duplicate the house pattern below onto yellow construction paper. Cut one per child.

WHAT YOU NEED

- ☐ house pattern from below
- ☐ one plastic jar with lid (peanut butter jar size) per child
- ☐ one rock per child
- ☐ sand or cornmeal
- ☐ hot glue gun
- ☐ 1/2-cup measuring scoop
- ☐ yellow construction paper
- ☐ glue

The Lord gives wisdom.
— Proverbs 2:6 (NIV)

Heralding Angel

This angel will teach the children that even though Jesus was born as a normal baby, His birth was special.

MEMORY VERSE

A Savior has been born.

— Luke 2:11 (NIV)

BEFORE CLASS

Cut an angel wings and head pattern (with halo and stem) from pages 31 and 32 for each child from yellow poster board.

Duplicate one angel face from page 31 per child.

Remove the tops from the detergent bottles, rinse them out, and dry well. The tops are not used for this craft.

WHAT YOU NEED

☐ angel head pattern from page 31
☐ duplicated angel face pattern from page 31
☐ wings pattern from page 32
☐ plastic dish detergent bottles without tops, one per child
☐ 12 x 10-inch foil sheets, one per child
☐ yellow poster board
☐ used fabric softener dryer sheets in pieces or cotton
☐ glue
☐ tape

WHAT TO DO

1. Give each child a piece of aluminum foil large enough to cover his detergent bottle (approximately 12 inches long).
2. Spread a small amount of glue over the bottle. Show the children how to mold the aluminum foil around the bottle to cover it.
3. Give each child the poster board figure of the angel's wings.
4. Spread glue on the wings and help the children cover the glue with pieces of used fabric softener dryer sheets.
5. Turn the wings over. Spread the other side of the wings with glue, and let the children cover it with pieces of dryer sheets.
6. Give each child a poster board angel's head and an angel's face. Spread glue in the middle of the head. Help each child place the angel's face on the head.
7. Show each child how to insert the stem of the angel head into the bottle.
8. Spread glue in the center of the angel wings. Help the children attach the wings to the bottles. Tape the wings, if necessary, for extra reinforcement.

✱ Say, **Jesus was born like all babies are born. But something very special happened right after He was born. An angel told some shepherds about His birth.** Let the children make their angels fly (at your cue) as you tell the story of the angel appearing to the shepherds. Then, say the memory verse together.

Bible Crafts On A Shoestring Budget

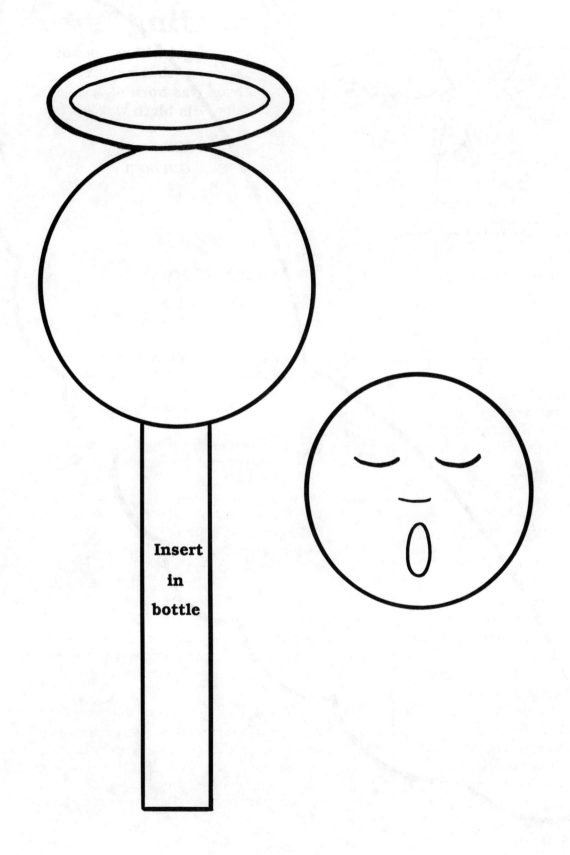

Insert in bottle

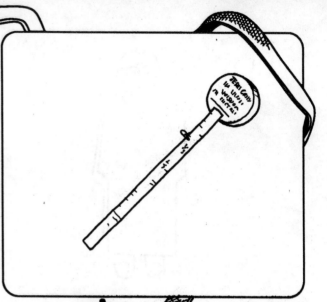

My Growth Tape

Preschoolers are very proud that they are growing. This chart will help them understand that Jesus grew, too.

MEMORY VERSE

Jesus grew in wisdom and stature.
— Luke 2:52 (NIV)

WHAT TO DO

1. Help each child slip a piece of ribbon through the slit in the plastic lid and glue a 1-inch flap to the back of the remainder of the ribbon.
2. Let the children place the memory verse circle on top of the plastic lid. Help them peel the backing off the adhesive-backed plastic circles (they will need help starting this) and stick it on the lid to cover the memory verse.
3. Hold each child's measuring ribbon against a wall so the end of the ribbon touches the floor. Mark his height and the date with a paper clip and/or a marker.
4. Say, **Jesus grew from being a small baby. At some point He was just your height. He did not stop there. He grew to be a man.** The children will appreciate the fact that once Jesus was just their size. Say the memory verse together.

TIP: If you use paste instead of glue, be sure to water it down and mix it well. This will make it easier for the children to use and will last longer.

Jesus grew in wisdom and stature.

—Luke 2:52 (NIV)

BEFORE CLASS

Cut a memory verse circle for each child. Cut circles from the adhesive-backed plastic to fit inside all of the plastic lids (approximately 3 inches in diameter), one per child.

Cut a slit near the edge of each lid through which the ribbon you are using will fit. Cut ribbon into 4-foot lengths.

WHAT YOU NEED

- ☐ duplicated circle pattern from below, one per child
- ☐ plastic lid from food container (approximately 3-inches in diameter), one per child
- ☐ clear adhesive-backed plastic
- ☐ 1 to 2-inch wide ribbon, 4 feet per child
- ☐ glue
- ☐ permanent marker

Jesus Helped

Use this finger puppet to help the children understand that Jesus looked at the needs of people and helped them.

MEMORY VERSE

They praised God.

— Matthew 9:8 (NIV)

BEFORE CLASS

Using the patterns on page 35, cut a poster board finger puppet, a paper memory verse box, and a cloth robe for each child. Cut finger holes in each puppet, as shown.

Draw a simple face on each puppet.

WHAT YOU NEED

- ☐ duplicated patterns from page 35
- ☐ poster board
- ☐ 2 1/2 x 5-inch or larger fabric scraps
- ☐ marker
- ☐ glue

WHAT TO DO

1. Give each child a puppet. Let each child choose a robe for his puppet.
2. Help each child glue his puppet's robe on the puppet. Do not let the glue extend below the top of the finger holes.
3. Give each child a memory verse box and help him glue it on the back of the puppet. Do not let it cover the finger holes.
4. Demonstrate how the children can make their puppets walk by placing two fingers in the holes of the puppet.

✱ Say, **Jesus saw a man who could not walk.** Have the children hold their puppets still — they cannot walk. **Jesus made the man able to walk again.** Let children move their fingers to make the puppets walk. **The people praised God because He helped the man.** Have the children say, **Thank You, God,** with you. Encourage the children to want to be like Jesus in desiring to help others. Say the memory verse together.

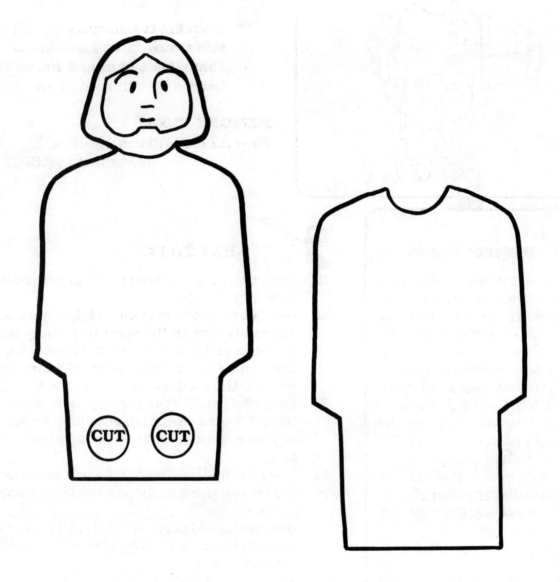

**They praised
God.**
— Matthew 9:8 (NIV)

Counting Book

This Bible counting booklet will teach twos and threes that Jesus can do a lot with a little.

MEMORY VERSE

They all ate and were satisfied.
— Matthew 15:37 (NIV)

BEFORE CLASS

Duplicate the basket pattern on page 37 onto tan or yellow construction paper, one basket per child. Cover the words on the pattern, and duplicate three more baskets onto brown paper for each child. Cut out the baskets.

Duplicate the pictures and memory verse box on page 37, one of each per child. Cut out the pictures and memory verse box and place them in piles so that matching pictures are together.

WHAT YOU NEED

☐ basket pattern from page 37
☐ duplicated pictures and memory verse from page 37
☐ brown construction paper
☐ tan or yellow construction paper
☐ chenille wire, 1/2 for each child
☐ marker
☐ hole punch

WHAT TO DO

1. Help the children practice counting from one to seven.
2. Say, **When your mommy and daddy cook a meal, I am sure they think about how many people are going to eat that meal. If there are a few people, they will cook a little food. If there are many people, they will cook a lot of food.**
3. Give each child four construction paper baskets (three brown and one tan or yellow). Be sure the tan or yellow one with Bible Counting printed on it is on top.
4. Let each child hold his four pages together while you punch two holes in the top left-hand corner of the booklet.
5. Help each child place half of a chenille wire through the two holes and twist. This will hold the pages together.
6. Handing them the pictures one at a time in order, help each child glue them on the proper pages. As they glue the loaves of bread on the first brown page say, **Jesus took seven small loaves of bread.** Let them point to the bread and count as you do the same. As they glue the fish picture on the back of the first brown page say, **Jesus also took a few fish and added His power** (let them glue the picture of Jesus on the second brown page), **and fed many, many people** (let them glue the picture of the crowd on the back of the second brown page).
7. Let the children glue the memory verse on the third brown page of their booklets. Write their names on the back cover. Say the memory verse out loud as they work.

Bible Crafts On A Shoestring Budget

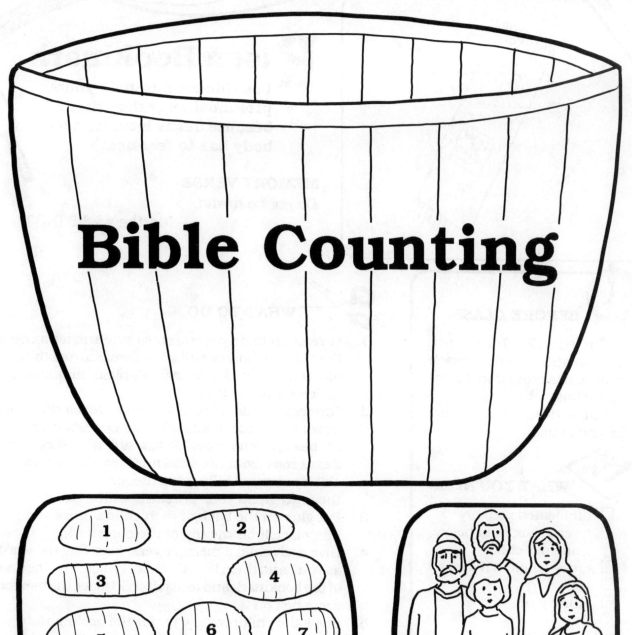

Bible Counting

loaves of bread +

many people fed

a few fish +

Jesus =

They all ate and
were satisfied.
— Matthew 15:37 (NIV)

The loaves are numbered 1 through 7.

Risen Bookmark

Use this craft to help your preschoolers realize that because Jesus is alive, nobody has to fear death.

MEMORY VERSE

Do not be afraid.

— Matthew 28:5 (NIV)

BEFORE CLASS

Cut a 1 1/2 x 7-inch strip of cross stitch fabric for each child. Cut a cross from felt for each child.

Cut a memory verse box for each child.

WHAT YOU NEED

☐ duplicated memory verse box from below, one per child
☐ cross stitch material
☐ felt
☐ fabric glue

WHAT TO DO

1. Give each child a piece of cross stitch material. Show the children how to pull a few threads from the ends of each piece of material. Explain that they are making a pretty fringe.
2. Give each child a felt cross. Say, **Jesus died on a cross so we could all have the opportunity to go to heaven one day. Jesus did not stay dead. Jesus rose from the dead and was alive again.** The children cannot fully grasp the concept of death, but they can grasp your peace about the subject.
3. Put glue on the back of each child's cross and help him place it on the top of the bookmark.
4. Give each child a memory verse box. Say the words as you hand them to each child. Put glue on the back of the bookmark and let each child place the memory verse box on it.
5. Show the children how to put the bookmark in the Bible or a Bible story book. Explain that they can mark their favorite stories or pictures with the bookmark.

Do not be afraid. — Matt. 28:5 (NIV)	Do not be afraid. — Matt. 28:5 (NIV)	Do not be afraid. — Matt. 28:5 (NIV)

Shadow Picture

Use this silhouette to help the children appreciate how wonderful it is that Jesus wants to be their friend.

MEMORY VERSE

You are my friends.

— John 15:14 (NIV)

BEFORE CLASS

Duplicate the memory verse banner pattern from page 40, and cut one per child. Cut pieces of brightly colored poster board to 8 1/2 x 11-inch or 9 x 12-inch size, one per child. Also cut a 1 1/2 x 9-inch poster board strip for each child, and fold it 1 1/2 inches from one end.

Use the silhouette pattern from page 40 to cut felt silhouettes of Jesus, one per child.

WHAT YOU NEED

- ☐ duplicated memory verse pattern from page 40, one per child
- ☐ bright colors of poster board, one 8 1/2 x 11-inch or 9 x 12-inch sheet per child
- ☐ 1 1/2 x 9-inch poster board strips, one per child
- ☐ dark felt
- ☐ glue

WHAT TO DO

1. Ask, **How does it feel when you find out someone wants to be your friend?** Let the children respond. Say, **I want to tell you about someone very special who wants to be your Friend.**
2. Place glue near the top of the poster board sheet and help each child cover it with the memory verse. Show the children how to smooth the paper over the glue.
3. Put glue on the back of the felt silhouette. Help each child place his silhouette under the memory verse on the poster board sheet.
4. Help each child tape the unbent end of the poster board strip to the back of the poster board sheet. Align the strip so that the fold of the strip meets the bottom edge of the poster board sheet. Show each child how to make the silhouette stand.
5. Say, **This is a shadow or silhouette of Jesus. Jesus is God's Son. Jesus loves you. He wants to be your Friend.**
6. Read the memory verse. Ask the children to say it with you as you point to the words.

Worship Doll

Making this doll will introduce the children to the privilege of worship and will help them revere God.

MEMORY VERSE:

Let us kneel before the Lord.

— Psalm 95:6

 WHAT TO DO

1. Let each child select a doll and a shirt.
2. Place glue on the doll's chest and help each child position the shirt in place.
3. Hand each child a chenille wire. Help him glue and tape the wire to the back of the doll so the "arms" wrap around in front of the shirt. Help him bend the arms so the hands come together as if in prayer.
4. Say, **God is so wonderful and great that we should always want to tell Him how much we love Him. We should always be ready to worship Him. We can show God how wonderful we feel He is by bowing our heads or kneeling before Him.**
5. Show your children how to bend the dolls at the knees to make them bow.
6. Read the memory verse. Ask the children to say it with you. Then, have them kneel and bow their heads and say it again.

 BEFORE CLASS

Use the patterns from page 42 to cut dolls from poster board and shirts from fabric scraps, one of each for each child.

Draw a face and a belt on each doll.

Bend both ends of a chenille wire approximately 90 degrees, leaving a 2 1/2-inch space in the middle. Bend the tips of the chenille wire 1/2 inch, to form hands. Do the same with each wire.

 WHAT YOU NEED

- ☐ patterns from page 42
- ☐ poster board
- ☐ 3-inch square fabric scraps, one per child
- ☐ glue
- ☐ marker
- ☐ chenille wire, one per child
- ☐ tape

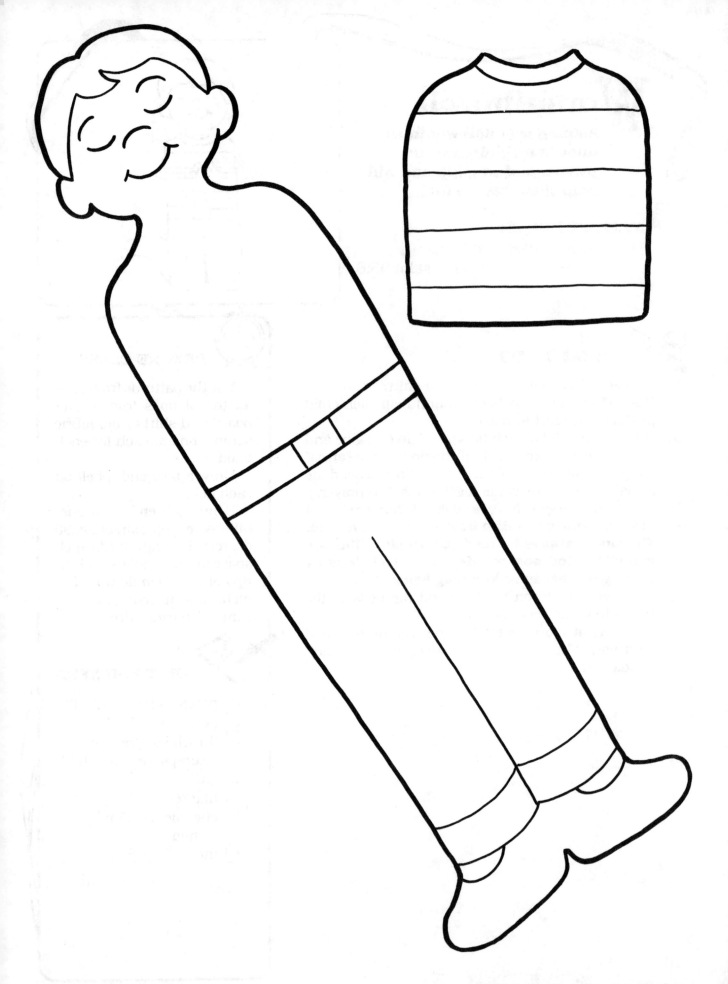

Praise Maker

Help your children experience the joy of singing praises to God using the instrument they make.

 MEMORY VERSE

Sing for joy to God.

— Psalm 81:1 (NIV)

 WHAT TO DO

1. Give each child a container. Let each child put several dried beans into the container.
2. Place the lid on the container and tape firmly in place.
3. Help each child wrap the adhesive-backed plastic around the container.
4. Let each child glue two or three musical notes and the memory verse onto the container.
5. Help each child twist two or three chenille wires (two with bells) together around the middle of the container.
6. Say, **When we sing praises to God, we can use our instruments to make rattles and jingling sounds.** Sing several songs with the children and let them shake their instruments. Then, say the memory verse together.

Sing for joy to God.
— Psalm 81:1 (NIV)

BEFORE CLASS

Cut a piece of adhesive-backed plastic to fit each container. Using the patterns below, cut musical notes from sheet music.

Duplicate a memory verse oval for each child and cut them apart.

Place a jingle bell on a chenille wire, move it to the center of the wire, and twist once to secure it. Make two chenille wires with bells for each child.

WHAT YOU NEED

☐ narrow cardboard or plastic cylinder with a lid for each child
☐ note pattern below
☐ duplicated memory verse pattern below
☐ chenille wire, 2-5 per child
☐ solid colors of adhesive-backed plastic
☐ jingle bells, 2 per child
☐ old songbook or music
☐ dried beans, 5 per child
☐ tape (colored optional)

My Prayer Sign

Children will learn that they can talk to God in prayer and that it's often helpful to have a special quiet place to pray.

MEMORY VERSE

Pray to your Father.

— Matthew 6:6 (NIV)

BEFORE CLASS

Using the pattern on page 46, cut a rectangle from bright poster board for each child. Cut the circle from the center.

Duplicate the smaller rectangle, the memory verse, and the diamond from page 47 onto contrasting colors of construction paper. Cut a rectangle, a memory verse, and a diamond for each child.

WHAT YOU NEED

☐ bright poster board
☐ patterns from pages 46 and 47
☐ adhesive-backed plastic or construction paper
☐ crayons
☐ glue

WHAT TO DO

1. Show the children the poster board hanger. Say, **Prayer is talking to God. We should each have a special quiet place to talk to God. You can put this hanger on your doorknob when you want to talk to God.**
2. Give each child a poster board hanger. Let the children scribble color the hangers.
3. Hand each child a small rectangle. Help him glue the small rectangle above the hole in the hanger.
4. Give each child a diamond. Help him glue the diamond just below the hole on the poster board hanger.
5. Hand each child a memory verse. Help him glue the verse at the bottom or on the back of the poster board hanger.
6. Say the memory verse with the children.

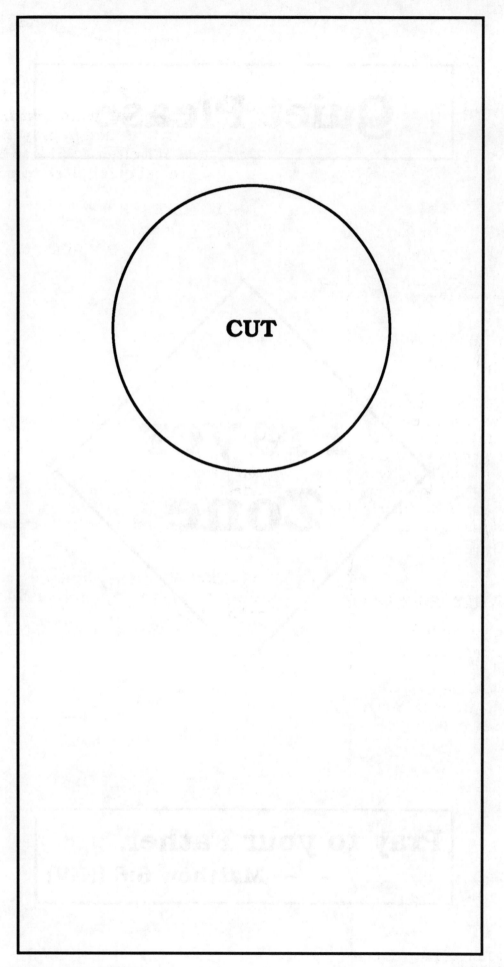

Quiet Please

Prayer Zone

Pray to your Father.
— Matthew 6:6 (NIV)

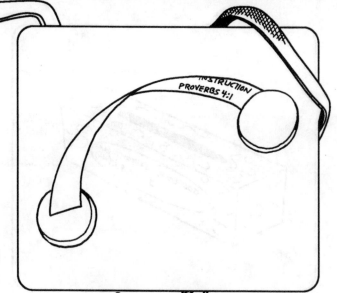

Silent Headset

This headset will help the children realize that God gave them ears for the purpose of listening.

MEMORY VERSE

Listen to a father's instruction.
— Proverbs 4:1 (NIV)

WHAT TO DO

1. Read the memory verse. Ask, **What part of your body do you use to listen?** Remind the children that God made their ears so they could hear.
2. Let the children glue one felt or poster board circle to each end of the plastic strip.
3. Give each child a memory verse box. Let him glue it on top of the plastic strip. Say the memory verse as you hand them out.
4. Show the children how to put the headsets on.

* Say, **God gave you ears. Use them to listen to wise people. Use them to listen to God's Word.** Encourage the children to use their ears to listen to stories from the Bible.

Listen to a father's instruction.
— **Proverbs 4:1 (NIV)**

BEFORE CLASS

Cut 1 1/2-inch wide rings from 2-liter plastic bottles. Each child will need one ring.

Cut each ring across its width, making a long, curved strip. Cut 3-inch circles of felt or fake fur. Each child will need two circles.

Duplicate and cut a memory verse box for each child.

WHAT YOU NEED

- ☐ duplicated memory verse pattern from below, one per child
- ☐ several 2-liter bottles
- ☐ 3-inch round scraps of felt or bright poster board, two per child
- ☐ permanent marker
- ☐ glue

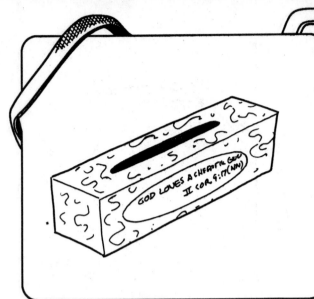

Giving Bank

Having a place to save some of his money for the church offering, can help a child develop a sense of giving.

MEMORY VERSE

God loves a cheerful giver.
— II Corinthians 9:7 (NIV)

BEFORE CLASS

Carefully unglue and flatten each box. Cut a money slot in one side of the box. Duplicate the memory verse pattern from below, one for each child.

WHAT YOU NEED

☐ one small cardboard box per child (toothpaste boxes are ideal)
☐ a penny for each child (optional)
☐ glue or tape
☐ crayons

WHAT TO DO

1. Let the children scribble color the inside of the boxes.
2. Read the memory verse. Say, **We should be happy to give some of our money to God. We should save some of the money we get to give to God.**
3. Help each child reconstruct his box, inside out, using tape or glue, placing the money slot at the top.
4. Give each child a memory verse and help him glue it on one side of the box.

✱ Point out the money slot and the memory verse on each bank. Say the memory verse as you point to the words. If you brought a penny for each child, show them how to put it in the bank. Give each child a penny, one at a time, and let him drop it in his bank as you say the memory verse.

God loves a cheerful giver.
— II Corinthians 9:7 (NIV)

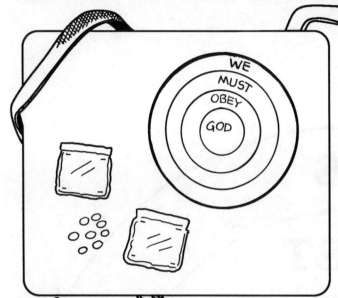

Obedience Toss

Making and playing this game is a happy way to impress upon the children the importance of obeying God.

MEMORY VERSE

We must obey God.

— Acts 5:29 (NIV)

BEFORE CLASS

Duplicate the target pattern on page 50 and cut one per child plus an extra.

Place a napkin in a plastic zipper bag with the napkin fold at the bottom of the bag. Open the napkin and staple half of it to one side of the bag and the other half to the other side, forming a pocket. Be sure that staple ends are inside the bag. Make one bag per child. Put 1/2 cup beans in a sock or nylon toe for each child and tie it securely.

WHAT YOU NEED

☐ duplicated target pattern from page 50
☐ dried beans or popcorn kernels in a large container, 1/2 cup per child
☐ threaded needle
☐ colorful 5-inch square or smaller napkins
☐ crayons
☐ plastic sandwich bags with zipper tops
☐ old socks or nylons

WHAT TO DO

1. Give each child a target to scribble color. Write the child's name on the back, and collect the targets. Say the memory verse words as they work.
2. Hand out zipper bags with napkins stapled inside. Let each child place a nylon or sock of beans in the opening of the bag.
3. Help each child close the zipper top tightly.
4. Show the target you made earlier. Read the memory verse on it once again. Say, **If we are to win in life, we must obey God.**
5. Place the target on grass or a rug (or tape it to the floor). Demonstrate how to throw the bean bag to try to hit the target. Let the children stand close to the target and encourage each child to try, one at a time, to hit it with his bean bag.
6. Ask each child to say the memory verse when he hits the target. Give each child his target and bean bag to take home.

WE

MUST

OBEY

GOD.

— Acts 5:29 (NIV)

Horn of Thanks

Use the time the children are working on this craft to talk to them about all the things they can thank God for.

MEMORY VERSE

Give thanks to the Lord.

— Psalm 105:1 (NIV)

WHAT TO DO

1. Give each child a cornucopia and two of each fruit pattern to scribble color.
2. Demonstrate how to weave the trash bag ties or chenille wires in and out of the slits in the cornucopia, weaving one tie or wire per column. (Do not be particular about how well they do this.) They may begin weaving each column on either side of the cornucopia.
3. Give each child a tie or chenille wire. Hand them a new tie or wire as they finish each column.
4. As they weave, say, **God gave us so many good gifts.** Name some things you are thankful for. Ask the children to do the same.
5. Hand the children one of each fruit, one at a time, beginning with the apple. Show them how to glue their fruit in the cornucopia opening, beginning at the top and working their way down.
6. Read the memory verse to them, then ask them to say it with you.
7. Hand each child a paper sack. Spread glue on one side of the sack and help the child glue the cornucopia to the sack. Make sure the cornucopia opening is at the open end of the sack.
8. Give each child three cardboard tubes. Hand him the three remaining fruit, one at a time. Help him glue each fruit onto a cardboard tube.

✱ Help the children stuff their paper sack with a sheet of tissue paper and place the cardboard fruit inside. Show them how the cornucopia rests on its side. Let them take out the fruit and stack it to match the fruit on the cornucopia. Say the memory verse together as you point to the words.

BEFORE CLASS

Use the pattern from page 52 to cut one cornucopia from poster board for each child. Cut slits or punch holes in each cornucopia as shown.

Duplicate the fruit patterns onto colored paper and cut them apart. Prepare two of each fruit for each child. Roll the top of each paper sack down 2-3 inches to form a rim.

WHAT YOU NEED

- ☐ patterns from pages 52 and 53
- ☐ brown or manila poster board
- ☐ trash bag ties or 4 1/2-inch chenille wires, 4 per child
- ☐ lunch size brown paper sacks, one per child
- ☐ tissue paper, one sheet per child
- ☐ 2-inch cardboard tubes, three per child (half a bathroom tissue roll)
- ☐ crayons
- ☐ glue

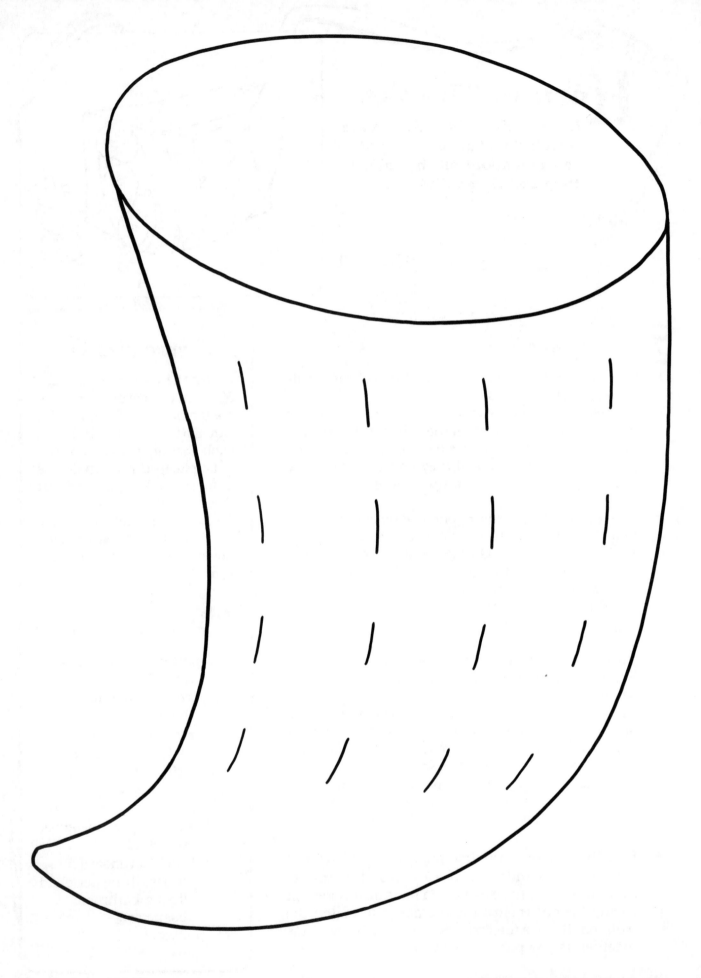

Give
thanks

to the

Lord.

— Psalm 105:1 (NIV)

Joy Ornament

Use this craft to help the children realize that Jesus' birth was part of God's big plan.

MEMORY VERSE

Jesus was born in Bethlehem.
— Matthew 2:1

BEFORE CLASS

Using the pattern on page 55, cut two ornaments for each child from poster board. Punch a hole in the top of each ornament, as shown.

From the sides of a two or three-liter bottle, cut circles using the circle pattern on page 55. On the plastic circles, print JESUS with a permanent marker.

WHAT YOU NEED

- ☐ ornament and circle patterns from page 55
- ☐ red and green poster board
- ☐ two or three-liter plastic bottles
- ☐ washable markers
- ☐ newspaper or a table cover
- ☐ permanent marker
- ☐ chenille wires, one per child
- ☐ hole punch
- ☐ scissors

WHAT TO DO

1. Give each child a poster board ornament. Allow each child to scribble color his ornament with washable markers. Protect the table with newspaper.
2. Place a thin line of glue on the uncolored side of one ornament piece.
3. Let each child place his plastic circle with JESUS written on it over the glue. Encourage him to hold it.
4. Place another thin line of glue on the plastic.
5. Help each child match the two sides of his ornament and glue them together. Encourage him to hold it until it dries.
6. As the children are holding their ornaments, say, **Jesus left heaven. He was born as a baby. We celebrate His birth on Christmas day. He did things we could not do so that one day we can be with Him in heaven. Jesus visited earth from heaven so that we can go to heaven someday, too.**
7. Give each child a chenille wire and help him push it through the hole in the ornament. Twist the ends to form a hanger.
8. Encourage the children to say the memory verse with you.

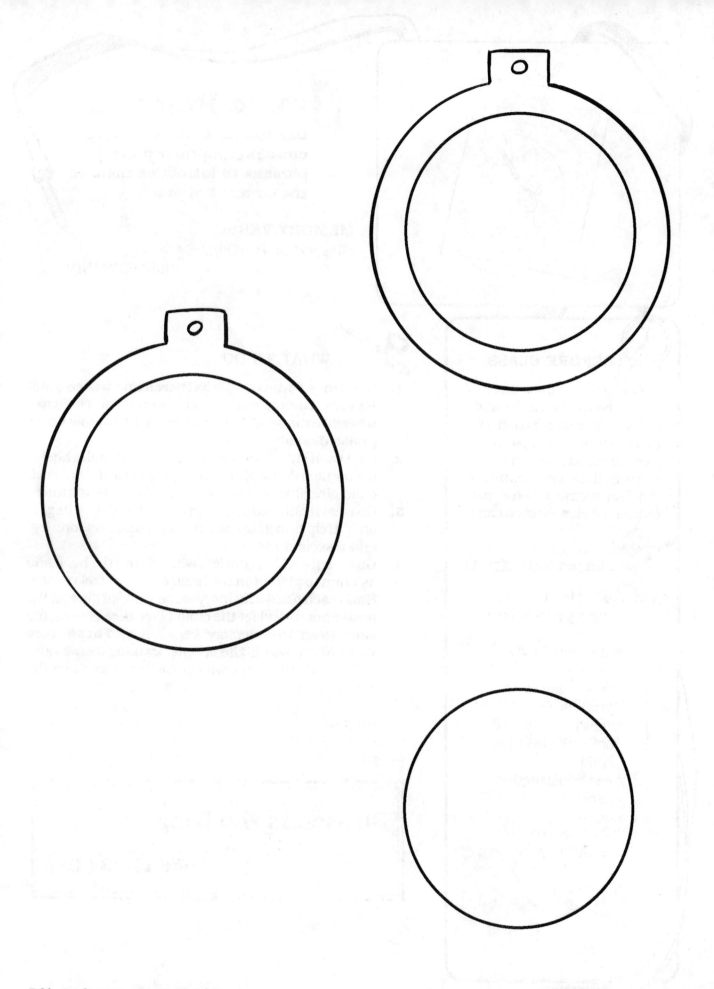

Praise Pretzels

Use the time the children are constructing their pretzel persons to introduce them to the concept of praise.

MEMORY VERSE

Blessed is the King.

— Luke 19:38 (NIV)

BEFORE CLASS

Cut a 6 x 8-inch piece of poster board for each child.

Using the illustration as a guide, cut a 4-inch palm leaf for each child. You may want to fringe it. Duplicate and cut out the memory verse pattern from below for each child.

WHAT YOU NEED

☐ duplicated memory verse pattern from below
☐ bag of small twist pretzels
☐ bag of small stick pretzels
☐ bright poster board, one half sheet per child
☐ green construction paper
☐ glue

WHAT TO DO

1. Say, **Once some people gathered and waved palm leaves. They placed palm leaves on the road where Jesus would ride to praise Him. How do we praise Jesus?**
2. Give each child two twist pretzels and a half sheet of poster board. Put glue on the pretzels and help each child place his pretzels as shown in the illustration.
3. Give each child one stick pretzel at a time with glue on it. Help him glue one arm, a second arm, one leg, and a second leg.
4. Give each child a palm leaf with glue on the back and ask him to place it in the hand of the pretzel person.
5. Hand each child a memory verse. Spread glue on the poster board and let the child place the verse on the glue. Read the memory verse. Say, **Those were some of the words the people praising Jesus said.** Talk about the ways we can praise God. Give the children a few pretzels to eat as you talk.

Blessed is the King.

— Luke 19:38 (NIV)

HE IS RISEN
MATT. 28:6

NAME _____

Easter Pop-Up

Making a pop-up tulip will help the children feel the joy that Jesus' friends felt when Jesus rose from the dead.

MEMORY VERSE

He is risen.

— Matthew 28:6

BEFORE CLASS

Duplicate the grass pattern from page 58 onto green construction paper, and cut one for each child. Duplicate the tulip pattern onto pastel paper. Cut one per child.

Cut paper or adhesive-backed plastic in 6 x 4 1/2-inch sheets, one for each child. Cut poster board into 1 x 10-inch strips, one per child.

Make a sample craft for the children to see.

WHAT YOU NEED

☐ duplicated patterns from page 58
☐ 4 1/2-inch cardboard tubes
☐ pastel wrapping paper or adhesive-backed plastic
☐ colorful poster board
☐ green construction paper
☐ pastel construction or copier paper
☐ tape
☐ glue

WHAT TO DO

1. Give each child a cardboard tube, and spread glue on it. Help each child cover his tube with wrapping paper.
2. Hand each child a tulip and a poster board strip. Let each child tape a tulip at the top of the strip.
3. Give each child a green grass pattern with his name on it. Help him glue the grass across the bottom of the poster board strip.
4. Help each child gently roll the sides of the tulip inward and insert it into the cardboard tube. Push the poster board strip until the pattern slides into the tube.
5. Demonstrate how to gently continue to push the poster board strip to make the tulip appear. The grass will prevent it from being pushed up too far.
6. Read the memory verse. Say, **Easter is a happy day because we remember that Jesus rose from the dead.**

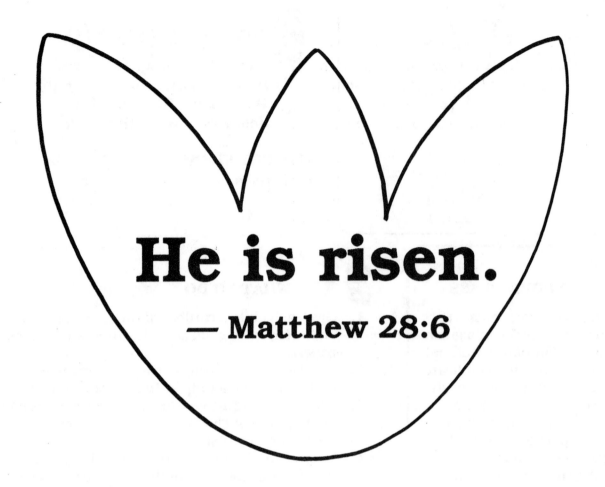

He is risen.

— **Matthew 28:6**

Name: _____

Fabric Heart

As the children work on this craft, talk about God's desire for them to love each other. Discuss ways to show love.

MEMORY VERSE

Love each other.

— John 15:12 (NIV)

WHAT TO DO

1. Say the memory verse. Say, **God wants you to love each other. What are some ways you can show love to each other?** Suggest ways the children can show love such as being kind, helping parents, sharing, etc.
2. Spread glue over each child's heart.
3. Encourage each child to cover the glue with pieces of fabric.
4. Give each child a memory verse pattern. Help him glue it to the back of the heart. Say the memory verse as you point to the words. Let the children say it with you.
5. When each child has finished, let the child run a twist tie through the hole. Twist to make a hanger.

BEFORE CLASS

Using the pattern on page 60, cut a heart for each child from poster board. Punch a hole in the top of each heart.

Duplicate the memory verse pattern on page 60 and cut one for each child.

Using pinking shears, if possible, cut the fabric scraps into small, irregular patches. Use as many textures and colors as possible.

WHAT YOU NEED

- [ ] duplicated patterns from page 60
- [ ] pink or red poster board
- [ ] small scraps of various fabrics
- [ ] glue
- [ ] twist ties from trash bags or chenille wire, one per child
- [ ] scissors
- [ ] hole punch
- [ ] pinking sheers (optional)

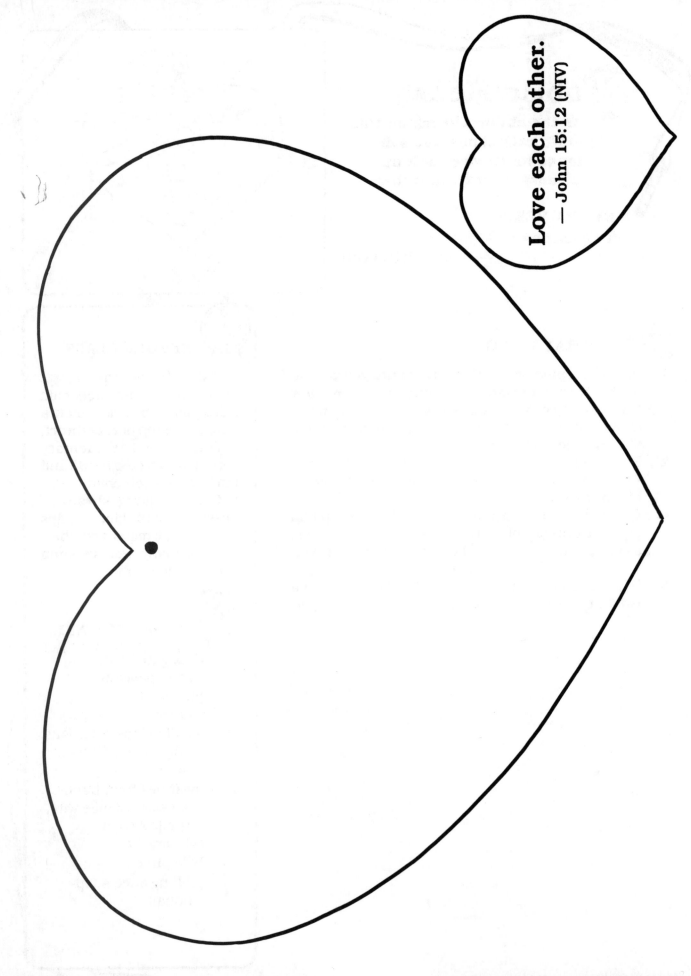

Love each other.
— John 15:12 (NIV)

Bible Crafts On A Shoestring Budget

Obeying Shapes

The children will learn about different shapes and will practice obeying as they make this hanging art.

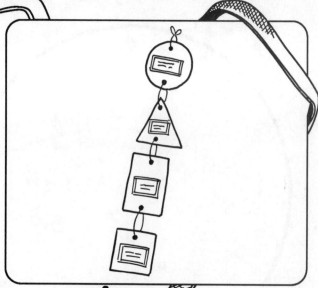

MEMORY VERSE

Children, obey your parents.
— Colossians 3:20

WHAT TO DO

1. Say, **The Bible says children should obey their parents. That means children should do what their parents tell them to do.**
2. Give each child a circle and two twist ties. Tell them to place a twist tie in each hole.
3. Help each child twist the top tie into a hanger and bend the bottom tie down to hold on to the circle (don't twist it yet).
4. Give each child a triangle. Show him how to attach it to the circle by placing the bottom twist tie of the circle through the top of the triangle.
5. Give each child a rectangle and a twist tie. Show him how to attach the rectangle to the triangle.
6. Give each child a square and a twist tie. Show him how to attach the square to the rectangle.
7. Arrange each child's hanging so the circle is at the top.
8. Give each child the word *Children* and help him glue it onto the circle. Give the children the remaining words, one at a time, and help them glue them on the appropriate shape: obey — triangle, your — rectangle, parents — square. Write the child's name on the back of the circle.
9. Say, **Because you obeyed me by following my directions, your hanging now says the memory verse.** Read the verse and ask the children to say it with you.

BEFORE CLASS

Cut one of each shape pattern on page 62 from different bright colors of poster board, one of each shape for each child.

Punch a hole in the top and bottom of each shape except for the square. It will only need a hole in the top.

Duplicate the words from page 63 onto colored paper. Cut one of each word for each child.

WHAT YOU NEED

- [ ] shape patterns from page 62
- [ ] duplicated word patterns from page 63
- [ ] bright colors of poster board
- [ ] trash bag twist ties or colorful chenille wire, four per child
- [ ] hole punch
- [ ] glue

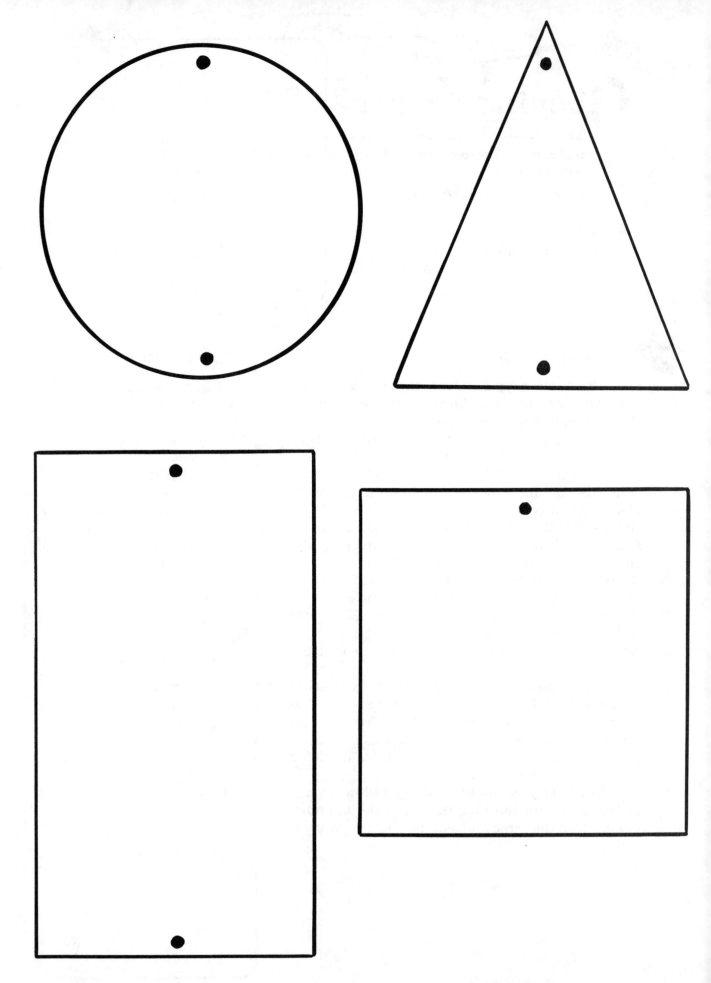

Children,

obey

your

parents.

— Colossians 3:20

More Bible teaching ideas that work!

Bible crafts for all ages

Children of all ages enjoy making these creative Bible crafts and learning Bible concepts, too. Each project comes with easy-to-follow instructions and a Bible memory verse and requires ordinary household materials. You'll find crafts for Sunday schools, VBS, children's church, and more.

Bible Crafts — Preschool RB36212
Bible Crafts — Grades 1 & 2 ....RB36213
Bible Crafts — Grades 3 & 4 ....RB36214
Bible Crafts — Grades 5 & 6 ....RB36215

Fun-to-make crafts teach Bible lessons

Even if they've never made a craft before, any teacher can successfully use these creative crafts to teach Bible lessons to children from age two through grade four.

Crafts are made with normal household items and come with step-by-step instructions, full-size reproducible patterns, Bible memory verses, and suggested guidelines for Bible lessons.

Creative Bible Crafts — Ages 2 & 3 ......RB36236
Creative Bible Crafts — Ages 4 & 5 ......RB36237
Creative Bible Crafts — Grades 1 & 2 ...RB36238
Creative Bible Crafts — Grades 3 & 4 ...RB36239

Order from your Christian Bookstore
Rainbow Books • P.O. Box 261129 • San Diego, CA 92196